Umbral

Maria Del Carmen Soto

Dedicated to

Aida Luz Reyes Carrillo

Table of Contents

Nameless
Poison
Rain
Sculptures Dawn
Return to Sender
Silent Darkness
Sorrow
Strangers
Struggle
The Dreamer
Time Heals
Umbra
Veil
Walls
We were
What Have I Done
What You Say
When Death Comes for Me
When You Left
When You Love
You Robbed Me
Your Tongue

Part III Penumbra
All the Same
Life
Little Liar
Lost
Love Lost
Loves End
More
Naked Moon
Strength is a Choice
Vintage Wine
Wear Your Crown

Part I Antumbra

Auburn Silhouette
Your auburn silhouette
Your onyx down
Your piercing flames
They enslaved my heart
One whisper from you held power over me
Silver rods and armor are futile in your presence
I am powerless and defeated
I crumble before you

Awe

Your beauty surpasses all standards
It is timeless, eternal
Your fragrance is inviting
An exquisite elixir

I stand before you in awe, heart unguarded, vulnerable

I long to be overcome by you
To be consumed by you
I long to savor you
To be by your side

Nothing is sweeter than your love

Bumble Bee

She was buxom and voluptuous
A curvaceous goddess
Petite in stature, giant in might

Feisty, a fighter in all sense of the word
Like David she brought down many Goliaths
Fearless and unintimidated Amazon

Her hands creators of delicacies
She was the salt of the earth
Our little bumble bee

Fierce Queen

She was a fierce queen, a warrior
She wore a crown of ebony silk and snow
Armor of grace and dignity dressed her frame

Her temple was a fortress
She was faithful, constant
Her dreams were mosaics of emerald walls and diamond floors

She had fists of steel and the strength of thousand men
Our mighty Amazon
Our forever rainbow queen

Lady Bug
She has coral lips
And eyes like piercing onyx
Her delicate skin
Soft like velvet

She wears a crown of ebony
Her hands are adorned with rubies, sapphires and pearls
Her curves are smooth and inviting
Her body sways like silk as she walks

All gaze at her beauty
It is timeless
It is breathtaking
Our captivating ladybug

Mother of Orphans

Olive complexion and skin soft like velvet
Mirrors of onyx and tresses of bronze
Your beauty is undeniable
It is obvious that you are royalty

You were bred from ardent amazons
You are a warrior of renowned fame
You wear a crown of fine diamonds
There is no other like you

You are the mother of orphans
Deity of compassion
Your heart made of pure gold
And your blood like a river of fire

Sisterhood

May my weaknesses be your strength
May my falls elevate you
May the obstacles that I overcome, pave your way

May every promise that was made over my life, be fulfilled in you
May every tear I shed, bring a thousand blessings over your life
May my journey through the desert, lead you to paradise

May my days of hunger and thirst bring you abundance
May my losses bring you victory
May my days of want, never knock on your doors

May my devotion bring favor over your life
May my lifting of you be multiplied in those to come
And when I die, may a part of me live through you

Stunning Queen

She was stunning
A royal with timeless beauty
A rose among the weeds

Heart of gold, fire in her blood
Brazen, unashamed and free
A femme fatale, stumbling stone to many

She was a rock, a sound foundation
Words were her delicacy
Love was her game
Our queen of stunning beauty

The Last Prince

A prince of great stature
Full of honor and strength
Of you, there aren't many
You're the last royal left

You built your own castle
With mortar and stone
The walls adorned with emeralds
The floors made of solid gold

You are a father to many
A prince to just one
Your mother was a warrior
And you her most beloved son

Last Remaining Queen

Mischievous amazon
Fearless and ferocious queen
Ruthless opponent
You are a force to be reckoned with
Elite warrior, the last of your tribe

No force, good or evil, dares to face you
You were sanctuary for those that perished
You taunted death and brought life
Death cannot touch you
It trembles in your presence

You are royalty
You are our rock
You give us strength
You are the root of our clan
Our last remaining queen

La última reina remanente
Amazona traviesa
Reina sin miedo y feroz
Adversaria despiadada
Eres una fuerza para tener en cuenta
Guerrera, la última de tu tribu

Ninguna fuerza, buena o mala, se atreve a enfrentarte
Fuiste santuario para aquellos que perecieron
Te burlaste de la muerte y trajiste la vida
La muerte no puede tocarte
Tiembla en tu presencia

Eres realeza
Tú eres nuestra roca
Tú nos das fuerza
Tú eres la raíz de nuestro clan
Nuestra última reina restante

Part II Umbra

Ataúd en Blanco

Ataúd en blanco
Mi vida ha sido como un ataúd en blanco,
Enterrado en terreno frio
Sumergido en lodo
Adornado únicamente por las flores silvestres y la yerba quemada
Fecha de nacimiento- incidental, matriz desconocida
Fecha de defunción- no digna de importancia
Contenido-
Un cadáver vacío
Demacrado y frágil
De forma insignificante
consumido por el rechazo
Cohibido de la humanidad
Desconocido por el amor

En fin, un ataúd, en blanco

Broken

With a broken heart,
And shattered dreams
The little girl lost all hope

With a festering heart
And haunting dreams
The little boy lost his soul

Together they walked
With no one to lead
With no heart to love and no dreams to dream

With no mercy to give
With no heart to cry
Will either of them live?
Will they both just die?

Burned

Our love was once passionate,
A fire raging through our souls
It consumed our thoughts, our desires, our every waking moment
You moved mountains to be with me, nothing else mattered
I was everything to you

The day came when it ended
The fire died out
Your thoughts were distant, and we were disconnected
My presence repelled you and my scent disgusted you
I was nothing to you

Your rejection pierced my soul
Your indifference destroyed my heart
As my chest caved in, all I felt was emptiness
I was consumed by pain
I hated myself for losing you

The day came when the rumors started
They said our love was yesterday's news, a thing of the past
They said our love was just a series of stale and outdated events
Now as I reflect on it all, our love was everything to me
Truth be told your love was like the tabloids; unreliable, fictional

Coffin

My life has been insignificant
Like a crude coffin
Buried in an unmarked grave
In cold terrain,
Submerged in filth
Adorned only by wildflowers and weeds
Date of birth- incidental
Date of death-not worthy of notice
Content-an empty vessel
An emaciated and frail corpse
Insignificant in its form
Consumed by rejection
Deprived of humanity
Unknown by love

My life has been irrelevant

Crown

Mommy raise your head up
Don't ever look down
There was nothing that you did wrong
You earned the diamonds on your crown

It was his demons that made him a monster
Not your blemishes or your ways
It was his evil that made him hurt us
Not your nurture or your praise

Mommy, I know you loved him
That the bruises brought you shame
And when you couldn't protect us
You felt anguish and endless pain

It was that monster that would hurt us
He would hide underneath our bed
He would wait in the darkness
And whisper secrets that caused us dread

Mommy, I know you loved him
It hurt you so much to see him dead
And when we saw your sadness
We wished that we had died instead

Darkness

In the darkness, the desert overpowers me
The devils claw tears through my sun-bathed bronze
And as the night fades, the once perfumed flesh wreaks of pestilence

In the darkness, the desert defiles me
The devils claw grinds down my sun-bathed bronze
And as my membranes wither, velvet becomes pelt

In the darkness, the desert consumes me
The devils claw devours my sun-bathed bronze and I become clay
The scent of death is upon me, and when the night is gone I will vanish

I Don't Fit In
As much as I want to deny it
The indisputable truth is, I don't fit in

A stranger among my friends
A foreigner in my country
A guest in my home
I don't fit in

I am a fish out of water
Off-beat, off-track, off
Eccentric, peculiar, alien
I don't fit in

As much as I want to deny it
The indisputable truth is, I don't fit in

Doubt

Looking back, we remember all the wars we fought
The broken hearts that we left un-mended
And all the hurt that we have caused

Time has backed out of our agreement
There are no contracts that can save us now
The sands are quickly flowing, time is running out

Tears and sorrow won't change this moment
There will be no mercy for us now
For the questions we incited, all the wonder led to doubt

Time won't give us reconciliation
There may not be mending of hearts
No chance to stop the hurting, no time to clear the doubts

Looking back, we remember all the wars we fought
And see that the greatest one remaining,
Is the one that doubt has wrought

Drawn to You

Why am I so drawn to you?
You are toxic,
Yet so delicious
You are poison
Yet irresistible

Why am I so drawn to you?
You are so ordinary
Yet so appealing
You are deadly
Yet so exciting

Why am I so drawn to you?
You consume me
Yet I long for you
You are evasive
Yet I seek you

Why am I so drawn to you?
You give me nothing
Yet I want you
You hurt me
Yet I forgive you

Why am I so drawn to you?

Eden

In Eden, our hearts were intertwined
I was sewn together in your womb
Your heartbeat was my lullaby
Your temple cradled me
Your joy was a symphony to my ears
And my heart rejoiced

When you wept, my soul cried out
Your tears moved me
Your soul's lamentation pierced me
Your agony tormented me
My soul wept
In Eden, our hearts will once again intertwine

Eyes Closed

When I close my eyes forever,
Will it break these treacherous reigns?
When I close my eyes forever,
Will I still feel this endless pain?
When I close my eyes forever,
Will my rage remain the same?
When I close my eyes forever,
Will it end all this shame?
When I close my eyes forever,
Will these bruises go away?
When I close my eyes forever,
Will they hear what I must say?
When I close my eyes forever,
Will these words be read that day?

Fairytales & Dreams

In my dreams
Life was sunshine
Strawberry fields and lavender scents
I dreamt of unicorns and castles
Crowns with rubies and emeralds

In my dreams
I danced in the rain
I counted the stars
I jumped in mud puddles
And I raced snails

In my dreams
Life was beautiful
Cherry blossoms dressed the sidewalks
Dandelions flirted in the fields
Ladybugs paraded their curves

When I awoke
Life went stale
The fields went baron
Unicorns became extinct
The castles became prisons
And the stars turned off

When I awoke
I could barely weather the storm
Crowns had thorns
The weeds poisoned the strawberry fields
And the sun would no longer shine

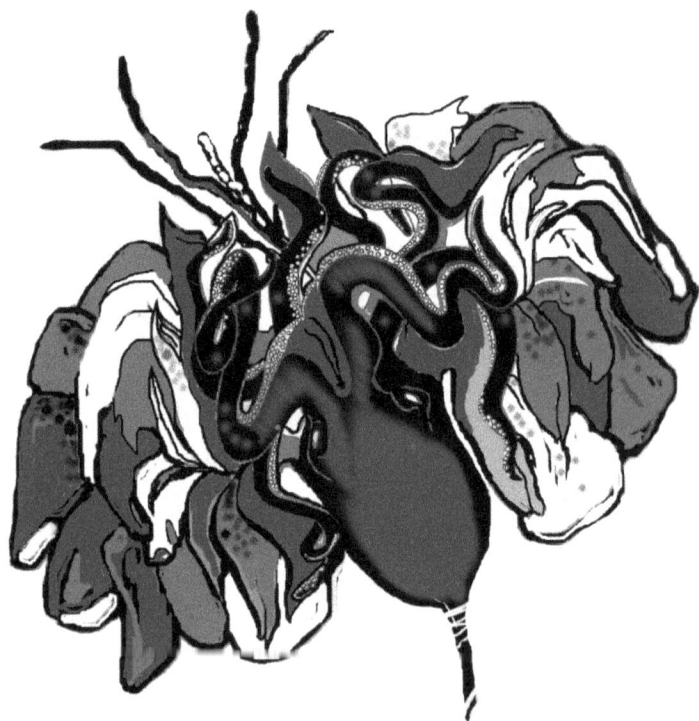

father why?

While I was in her womb
Your first kiss was a bruise
Like a serpent thrashing at my mother's heals
Like a reaper collecting a soul
You were merciless

I often wanted to ask, 'father why?"

When I was born
You denied me a name
You refused to give me an identity
You negated my birthright
You deemed me unworthy to be called "daughter"

And as I grew
I would interrogate my heart
I thought the answer lied deep within its chambers
Perhaps the answer was in my DNA
Yet I drew a blank

I often wanted to ask, "father why?"

Your rejection pierced my soul
It traveled deep into my inner being
It stole every drop of hope left within me
It strangled my faith in humanity
For a long time, I felt empty

As you fought against your demons, you became a monster
All I was to you, was a sacrificial lamb
The bruises were not as painful as your words
You let me believe that I was unworthy of compassion
I wasn't good enough to be "daddy's little girl",

Did you hate me because I was ugly?
Perhaps my complexion offended you?
Or was it my frail, emaciated form that displeased you?
You convinced me that I was definitely not created in your image
I certainly wasn't enough to be called "daughter"

When you were gone
I knew that I would never get my answer
I would never know the truth
I would roam the Earth with the same taunting question
And I could never ask "father why?"

Fear

Fear, you're a wicked liar
Eden's serpent in disguise
You feast off of our sorrow
You plan for our demise

Fear, you're a cannibal
Feasting on our dreams
You have but one true passion
To tear us open at our seams

Fear, you're a back-stabbing traitor
How I wish that you were dead
Next time you retaliate you monster
May they place a ransom on your head

Fear, you're another false prophet
You plan to steal our starving souls
You make claims of fame and profit
Hiding the sorrow, you impose

Fear, I long for your departure
How I wish that you were dead
Covered in dirt and hungry maggots
May scavengers sever off your head

Guillotine

Like the guillotine, my words are
Sharp, vicious, deadly blades
They storm through me swiftly
They contaminate my heart
They are saturated with poison

With contempt, my words lash out
Piercing souls, bringing death
I have no restraint, no discipline
I am powerless over the rage that they possess
As they flow from my inner core, they leave carnage behind

My words sow decay and reap death
I am paralyzed by the power that they bare
Yet they intrigue me
Their darkness and death seduce me
Their violence consumes me

Like the guillotine, my words are
Widow-makers
Orphan-makers
Bringers of death and destroyers of life
They are the guillotine

Hopelessness

Hopelessness, exhaustion
They dwell within me
They spread through me like wildfire
The longer they stay the more difficult it is to stand
I fall to my knees

Disgust, sorrow
They move within me
They suffocate me as each day passes
As they grow they diminish my strength
And as I fall to my knees, it all seems more hopeless

Void, emptiness
They thrive within me
They diminish me to a residue of what I once was
As they consume me they reduce me to an empty shell
And as I try to stand, I fall

Hyena

I don't understand your ways
At times you demonstrate kindness
You give freely, generously
Then, in a blink of an eye, you snatch it all back

There are moments that you are gentle
Your kindness radiates from within
You are soft, happy
Then in a bat of an eyelid, you take it all away

Like the hyena, you are a scavenger
Preying on the hearts of the more vulnerable
Devouring the remaining humanity of those lost
Your cackling laughter constant and mocking your victims

You are worthy of contempt
You are feral and unrestrained
You feed on the carcass of those that love you
Like the hyena you are unpredictable

I am enough
Although the years have passed
And I am worn
I am enough

Although my skin is no longer velvet
And my crown is ebony and snow
I am still enough

Although my windows are clouded
And my pearls are tainted
I am still enough

I am undeserving of comparison
I am worthy of loyalty and praise
I am enough

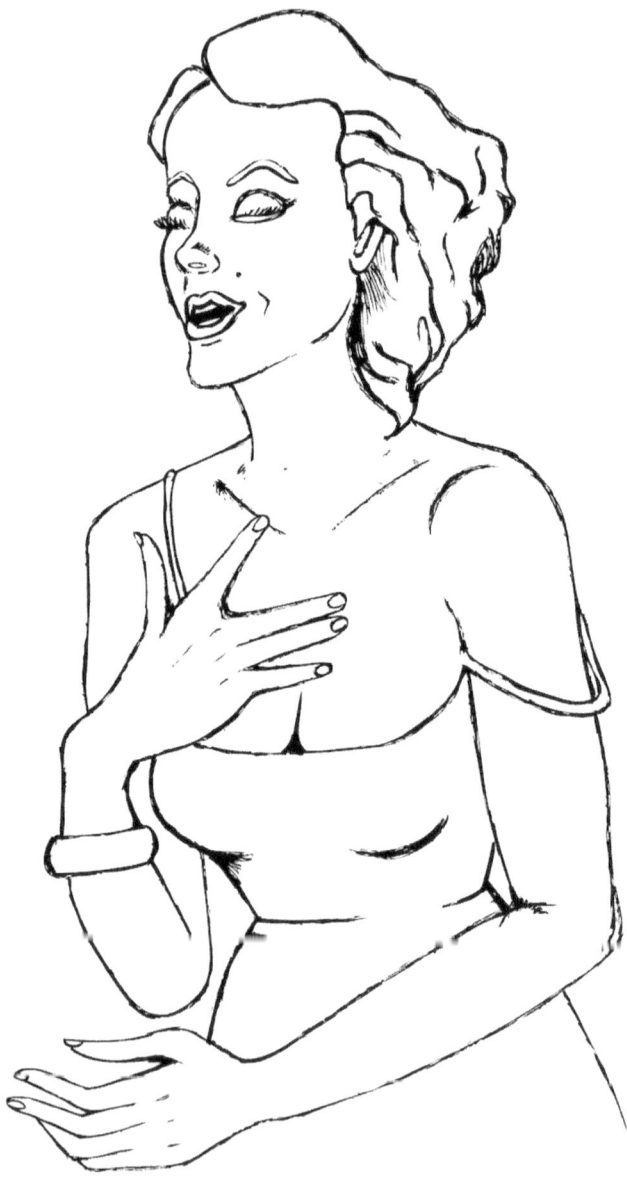

I Gave You My Life

I gave you my life
Yet you despised me
You were made to bring me death

Your sole purpose
To shame me
You strip me of my dignity

You turn your back
You tried to smite me
You brought pestilence to my temple

I have nothing left for you
There is nothing else that you can take
Yet you are determined to steal what I no longer have

Imperfect

Yes!
I am imperfect

Flawed in many, many ways
Blemished and asymmetrical
Sometimes I dance offbeat
Sometimes I color outside of the lines
Sometimes my voice cracks when I sing
Sometimes I go Up the stairs on the Down side

Yes!
I am imperfect

In Anticipation

I wait in anticipation for the moment that you will
Abandon the charade,
Concede to the truth,
Reveal your true intent

I want to see you expose your true nature, your secret identity
You are a wolf in sheep's clothing
You are a lion in the lamb's skin
You are nothing but a deceitful coward

You thrive on demoralizing the humble
You trample on the fragile
You mock the weak
You scavenge on the carcass of those that loved you

It Could be

There was once a young girl
She had a dream
It was of the perfect kingdom
Of which she would be queen

She was encouraged to dream
To believe in what could be
To reach high for the stars
And as deep as the sea

As she faced the unknown, she was true, in her heart
She gave her Father honor, she set herself apart

The young girl became queen
She had honor and prestige
And as the story goes, when she grew old
She was worth more than rubies and gold

There was once a young boy
He was unable to dream
He had a kingdom
Of which he was king

He was forbidden to dream
Told to stay on the ground
To believe in what he can see
Lean only on what he had found

As he faced the unknown, He was weak in his heart
He took all the honors, and his kingdom fell apart

The young boy became dismayed
He lost his kingdom and his way
And as the story goes, when he grew old
He walked alone for the rest of his days

Mere Vessel

I am a mere vessel
Molded by a master artisan
Exquisite in his eyes
Yet imperfect in my own

My flaws take his breathe away
Yet my mistakes suffocate me
His perfect hands mend my broken heart
As my head drops in shame, he lifts it up

When I think that I have reached the end of my journey
He paves new paths for me
Some paths are laid with thorns and rough terrain
Others will solid ground of brick and mortar

I am worn and tattered
A broken vessel that has lost its beauty
Yet he adorns me with silk garments and a crown of diamonds
His love is a mystery to me, it's inexplicable

Nameless

I am not glorifying your name
In my eyes you are an abomination
You should forever crawl on your belly
So that I may stomp on your head

I am not acknowledging your identity
In my eyes, you are unworthy
You are a vampire and you should be subject to their laws
Perish when you enter without invitation

I am not honoring you as a nation
In my eyes, you are hostile, dishonorable vipers
You invade our temples and kill our first born, taint our legacies
You should be sterilized so that you can no longer reproduce

I am not dedicating these words to you
In my eyes you are null, invalid, a coincidence
These words honor those you have smitten
So that in their strength you can become weak.

Poison

Your lips spewed the poison
That my unguarded heart devoured
When the rage soared through my veins
My soul rejected it
My inner being became tainted
My thoughts were vile and cluttered
As I bit my lips and clenched my fists
My soul jumped about
It became enraged and bitter
Turmoiled at its inability
To guard its most prized possession
Its heart

Rain

As the rain falls it dampens my soul
With every drop that falls upon me, I feel comfort
The dark clouds make me feel at home
And I finally fit in

The rain attempts to cleanse me
Yet I corrupt it
My darkness pours out, its sinister intent is absorbed by the drops
The rain is no longer pure

The darkness dances around me
It is a witness that I exist
It courts my soul and at the end
It mocks me because it knows that I am not alive

Yet the rain it comforts me….

Sculptures Dawn

Your sculptures dawn was
Voluptuous, enticing, desirable
With its step, your flirtatious perfume slayed
Giants fell, and you were fierce.

Your sculptures sunset was
Dampened, weary, clumsy
With its step, your scent was no longer felt
You held no power, you were worn

Your sculptures night was
Thin, un-moving, diminished
With its step, your scent inspired no more
Giants mourned, and you were no more

Return to Sender

The Elders say that words have authority,
Words have power and dominion over our lives
I declare that your words are rubber daggers
They are harmless movie props
Unsophisticated
Obsolete
Primitive weapons
They have no power over me

Your words are isolated echoes on a deserted isle
Fractured hiccups that go unheard
They are limp scarecrows that have lost their scare
Ridiculous lyrics that disperse the crowds
Your words have no rhyme, no reason

Your words are feather-weight cannons that bounce off my walls
Your words hold no dominion over me
I reject them and condemn you to silence
I return them to you stamped "Deliver to someone who cares"

Your words are returned to sender....

Silent Darkness

In the silent darkness
My soul cries out to its first true love
My seams are coming apart
The poisons of humanity surge through my veins
The bitterness and anger have imprisoned my heart
I am worn
I am decomposing in the bile and stench of human intent
In silence I crave for death, the darkness devours me

My soul cries out to its first true love
I question my creation
I am vile, imperfect, ugly
My skin wreaks of decay
My limbs are waning
My lips spew death
In the silent darkness, my soul cries out to its first true love
and I can no longer hear his response...

Sorrow

As she sees my sorrow
The blood moon cries
As she sees my hunger she moves the oceans
Her sobs make the Earth tremble
She's drawn to me like a mother who has just lost her child
Her embrace consoles me as she gently rocks me
The wicker cradle offers no sanctuary

My hunger rages through my being
Sugar water saturates my pallet, it offers no relief to my hunger
Her tears bathe me
She knows that she holds in her arms a living sacrifice
A child to be devoured by the god
Her embrace offers a penetrable fortress
A tower that could not shelter me

Before the blood moons' eyes, the god will rip me from her arms
In the darkness, my flesh will be torn from my bones
There will be gnashing teeth, a mouth bathed in my blood
My blood will be a delicacy that entices savagery
The god will scream in delight

The blood moon will mourn.......

Stranger

As we walk down the street
Who is the stranger?
When we lie, and we cheat
Who is the stranger?

A stranger isn't always an unknown
It can be a lover or a foe
Someone you already know, is a stranger

You see the face, not the hearts
That mask will tear you apart
They can share your bed
Say they love you, but hate you instead

Someone you already know, is a stranger

Struggle

There is a struggle within me
A fight between the good and the evil
They are fighting over the dominion of my soul
The balance that once existed has been disturbed

As I starve the evil it becomes more rabid
With each passing day its' hunger increases
The need to survive turns into an overpowering primal instinct
Its transformed into a fierce and reckless force

As I feed the good it becomes docile
With each passing day its flames are dying down
And as it sees the strength of evil it cowers
Its transformed into a benign force and goes dormant

The evil is now feral
It is savage and uncontrollable
It unleashes words of death without hesitation
Their venom brings destruction

The good is now fading away
It is paralyzed, debilitated
Unable to strike down the enemy
It is now powerless over any weapon forged by evil

To avoid persecution, my soul must suppress the struggle
It must resuscitate the good and tame the evil
All it can do for now is wear a mask of gentle kindness
To live, it must betray the champion

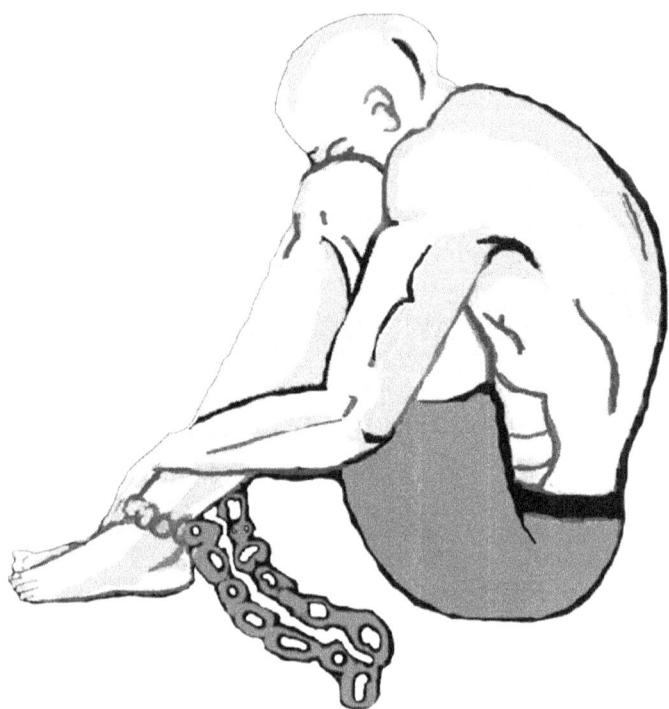

The Dreamer
You are the subject of conversation
The talk of the town
As you walk by the crowds, they can't help but to stop and stare
There are times you think it's in admiration and others in envy
What you don't know is that you are the subject of ridicule

They see you as a naïve dreamer
You have told them you seek romance
That you dream of true love
You fantasize about rose petals laid perfectly on your silk sheets
What you don't know is that dreams aren't real

Your insatiable desire for companionship inspires pity
Your desire for love goes unfulfilled
You are vulnerable, and it makes you weak
You are trusting, and it makes you easy prey
You are so thirsty

What you don't know is that dreams are just glorified nightmares
What you don't know is that reality is ruthless
What you don't know is that life is merciless
What you don't know is that love is a myth
What you don't know is that happiness is a fairytale

Time Heals

I hear that time heals all wounds
Explain how time will heal a dead child
Explain how time will mend the soul of a mourning mother
Explain how time will piece together that broken heart

Time doesn't heal anything
If unattended pain festers within your heart
It becomes malignant and deadly
The broken heart begins to rot

The idea that time heals all wounds is a façade
It is a smokescreen used to hide reality
It is camouflage used to conceal the pain yet to come
But in the end, the truth is revealed

I hear that time will tell
Time seems to be a gossip and nosey body
The truth is time is unkind
It steals your youth and robs you of your life

Time is a dictator that can never be overthrown
It is a tyrant and an oppressor that takes it all
Time loves no one and fears nothing
It is a ruthless thief and has no remorse.

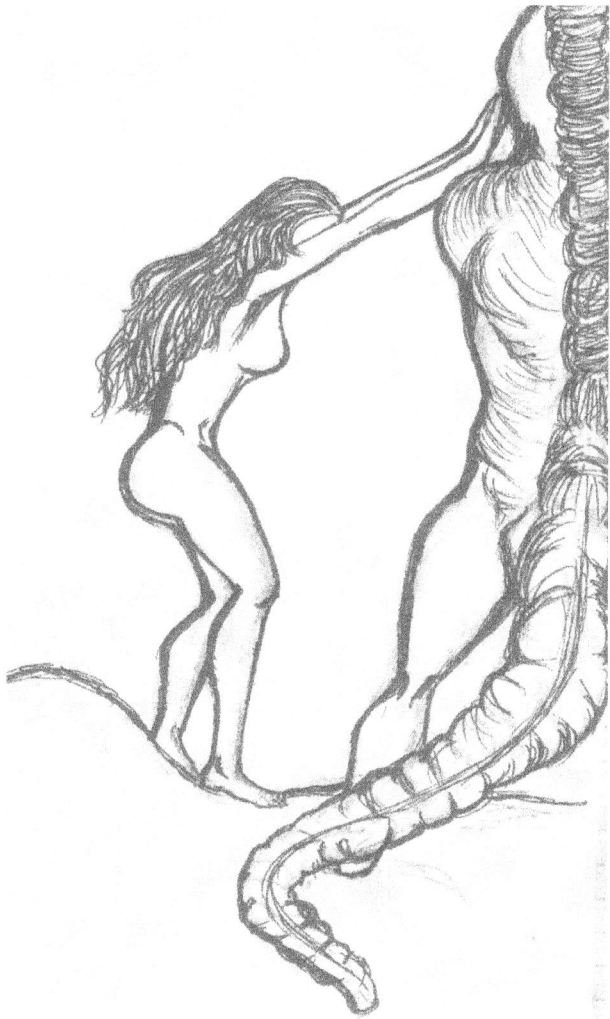

Umbra

There is no more light left in me
All that remains is a shadow
The darkness is all that I can see
It penetrated my very marrow

There are no lamps to light my path
Just stumbling stones along the way
The stars can see my burning wrath
And they refuse to guide my way

What was once an ardent and fiery light
The path has blown away
I'll walk in dark and endless nights
Throughout the rest of my days

Veil

I stand before you without a veil
My heart unguarded
Betraying reason, defying my will
I surrender before you
Yet you reject me
Your words pierce my soul
I humble myself before you and you disgrace me
Your anger is unconcealed
Your cowardice disgusts me
Yet I am drawn to you
I loathe you
Yet I submit to you

Walls

Damp, dark walls close in on me
A prison of smiles and kind gestures
I suffocate in my own hypocrisy
Well-rehearsed lies keep me living

"Love", "loyalty", "family" all around me
Still, I am irrelevant, an extra, a fill-in
I am empty
I am invisible

My thoughts ridicule me
They dare me to reveal my truth
Promises of love and happiness enter my mind
Who is the fool now?

I will always be invisible

We were

We were
    Two children
    Embracing each other
    Believers in the power of love, kisses and sweet dreams,
    Longing for magic and strawberry fields forever
    Seekers of Eden
We were
    Awakened by the cruelty of this world
    Stalked by darkness
    Preyed on and defeated by fear
    Assaulted by reality
    Two hopeless nobodies
    Without identities, fragile phantoms in this world,
    Hidden in plain sight
    Incidental, obsolete, and redundant souls
 We were
    Figments of the imagination,
    Unwanted and destitute,
    Meaningless casualties
    Dwelling in the filth and vile of humanity
    Little houses with dim windows
We were
    Gone but never reported missing
    Trampled by life and mocked
    Ridiculed by society
    Devoured by pestilence
We were
    Nothing

What Have I done
What have I done?
I have brought up charges against those that offend me
Condemned those that wronged me
Yet I have overlooked my own iniquities

What have I done?
I have sheltered my failures
Harbored resentment
Yet I too have inflicted pain on so many

What have I done?
I have re-payed kindness with hate
Turned people against each other
Yet I continue to glorify my pain at the expense of others

What have I done?
I too have pierced hearts
And like the serpent, I have stolen Eden
My lips have spilled poison
My words have brought death

What have I done?

What You Say

You say you love me
That I am perfectly imperfect for you
That I am voluptuous and fierce
The temple you adore

You say you love me
That my scent is exquisite
That my lips arouse you
And that my skin tastes like ambrosia

You say you love me
That I will be your one and only
Your exclusive muse
The saint of your devotion

You say you love me
That I am your true love
That there will never be another
And that you would die for me

I say that those are just words

When Death Comes

When death comes for us
Will we greet her with a kiss?
Will we invite her in?
Will we recognize her?

We know that tomorrow was never promised
We are just passing by
Special guests on a short-term trip
Before we know it, death will escort us home

Our inner-most dreams are of an eternity in paradise
The thought of sleeping indefinitely strikes fear in our hearts
We are horrified at the idea that our soul will die
Contemplating a final death is terrifying

When death comes for us
Will we greet her with a fight?
Will we hold on to life and stand firm?
When death comes for us, will we stand a chance?

When You Left
When you left,
The birds gave up there singing
The wind refused to chime
The flowers cried and wilted
The fields grew baron and dry
The horizon fell over and tilted
Nature decided to die

When you left,
The earth started to tremble
The mountains began to roar
The oceans they rose and resounded
The trees grew weary and sore
The eagles were stricken with madness
The deserts they closed all their doors
The valleys collapsed in deep sadness
Nature could take it no more

When you love

When you love,
You don't put up walls , because love must not be contained
You don't hide your heart, because love is transparent
You don't lie, because love is truth
You don't assault, because love is kind
You don't force, because love is a choice

When you love,
You give all of you because love is fueled by generosity
You protect it because love needs to be guarded
You confess it because love needs to be known
You treasure it because love is more valuable than silver and gold
You surrender it all because love is worth it.

You Robbed Me

I woke up one day to find that you robbed me
Of all people you robbed me
You took my most prized possession

You made me fall deeply in love, so that there could be no other
You let me dream of us and yet there was only you
You forced me to sacrifice my dreams so that you could fulfill yours
You allowed me to go with want so that you could have it all
You turned me into a servant so that you could be my master
You took my dignity to make me submissive to you
You snatched my laughter so that only you knew happiness
You forced your hand to make me fear you
You stole my confidence to make me humbled before you
You hid me from all so that my world became small

I woke up one day to find that you robbed me
You took my most prized possession
You took me

Your Tongue
Your tongue is like….
Devils Claw gashing, ripping the flesh off its prey
The Bubonic Plague devouring civilization
Famine enslaving a village of the destitute
Cannibals set free upon tribes of helpless children
Piranhas in a pond of goldfish
Medusa enticing the frail hearted among men
Crystal Meth raging through an addict's system
The Serpent snatching paradise from man

Your tongue is carnage

Part III Penumbra

All the Same

As strangers walk by and greet with, "how are you?"
The response is always the same
As the room fills with friends they all ask, "how are you?"
The response is always the same
"I am doing great thanks"

It's all the same,
Strangers and loved ones
Friends and foes
It's all the same

I am imprisoned in a tomb
I am imprisoned in a forgotten mausoleum
I am imprisoned in an unmarked grave
Life is loneliness and loneliness is life
It's all the same

The loneliness is crippling
Am I alive or do I merely exist?
Am I dead or do I merely die a little every day?
It's all the same

Life

Life is fragile and so precious
We fall hopelessly in love with her
We crave her magnificence
We savor her taste and are intoxicated by her fragrance

We believe we are giants and worthy to dwell with her
We entice her with our passions
We seduce her with our ways
We trust that she will be with us tomorrow

Why do we believe that we are immune to her enchantments?
Why do we believe that we are invincible to her power?
Why do we feel that we are indispensable, a necessity?
Why do we think we are her master?

We are blind and naïve to the truth
We bring destruction to her
We are reckless and insignificant
We are arrogant to believe that we are essential

The reality is that we will perish
Once our life is diminished, death will erase our existence
Our days will be casual memories
It must be that way

We are presumptuous beings
We fail to realize that tomorrow was never promised
We are simply passing by
In a blink of an eye, life will extinguish us

Why do we wonder what our soul will see when death comes for
us? Why not enjoy what it saw in life?
Why do we wonder if our vessels will perish beautifully or
abruptly? Why not admire its' beauty now?
Why do we mourn our death prematurely? Why not enjoy our life?
Why do we fear our end? Why not make our life count instead?

Life seems fragile and that is what she wants us to believe

Little Liar
Should I believe your words
Little liar
Should I hold on to your promises
Little liar

If being a liar became an occupation
You would the first in line with your resume
You would be the guru of lies
Its patron Saint

You breathe, sleep, and eat lies
They are your favorite entree
Your most desired dessert
You serve them warm and cold alike, little liar

Is everything you cast off a lie?
Is your reflection a lie?
Please don't answer, of course, it is a lie
It's all a lie, little liar

The elders revered truth and abhorred lies,
They spoke of the destruction of lies
But you are immune to the ways of the elders
You abhor the truth and embrace lies

Oh, what a shame, little liar
You mock traditions, values, and life
You embrace death, destruction, and lies
Oh the tears we have shed for you little liar

Lost

In my darkest hour, I lost my way
It was the pain and the doubt
It led me astray
And although I fought like a warrior, with might and grace
When it really mattered, I lost my way

In my darkest hour, I lost my way,
It was the rain and the drought,
It led me astray
And although I held on to avoid disgrace
When it really mattered, I lost my way

In my darkest hour, I lost my way
It was shame and temptation
It led me astray
And although I said I wouldn't sway
When it really mattered, I lost my way

Love Lost
My heart can no longer love
It is defiled
It is desecrated

My iniquities have severed its lifeline and now
Sorrow has infested its chambers
Through it flows maggot-ridden rivers

Rot and pestilence have replaced compassion
All that remains is the stench of the rancid waters
And its demise is delivered slowly as agony reigns its last days

Love Ends

The thought that our love can end
Suffocates me
The thought that it is a thought in your mind
Tortures me
The thought that this is not true love
Destroys me

More

There has to be something better
There has to be more to life

All the pain has to lead to healing
All the sorrow has to lead to happiness
All the fighting has to lead to reconciliation
All the hunger has to lead to an abundance
All the guilt has to lead to redemption
All the ugly has to lead to beauty
All the tear shedding has to lead to cries of laughter
All the death has to lead to life

There has to be something better
There has to be more to life

Naked Moon

The nakedness of the moon hypnotizes me
It is her glorious glow that captures my attention
Her lips want to reveal her secret but she holds back
Her eyes penetrate my soul and she knows it
I am intoxicated by her beauty

When her silhouette is clothed with a diamond-studded dress
Her dark cloak conceals my sadness
It is in her embrace that I find true rest
Her song comforts me
Her whispers are my lullaby

Her visits quench my thirst
Hints of her departure fill my heart with dread
And the threat of losing her breaks me
All of me longs for all of her
She has absolute power over me

My heart has but one question, does she long for me as well?

Strength is a Choice

Strength is a choice
The choice to show compassion even towards those that demonstrate no empathy
The choice to show mercy even towards the merciless
The choice to remain silent when your words will bring death
The choice to rise after being knocked down
The choice to love although hating is easier
The choice to smile when you are really crying inside
The choice to embrace when you really want to strike
The choice to let go when you really want to hold on
Strength is a choice.

Vintage Wine

Your love is like vintage wine
Sweet and desired
But too costly for the common folk

Your love is like vintage wine
Intoxicating, dangerous, scarce

Your love is like vintage wine
Too rich for my blood, restricted
Out of my reach

Wear Your Crown

When you wear a crown
You lace it with rubies and diamonds
You don't tarnish it or wire it with thorns

When you wear a crown
You carry yourself with honor
You elevate, you build, you inspire

When you wear a crown
You lift those that have fallen
You empower, and you sow

When you wear a crown
You speak from your heart's abundance
You use words to help others grow

When you wear a crown
You recognize royalty
Queens call out to queens

A message from the author

I was hesitant to publish Umbral because of what people would say. The fear of negative feedback was crippling. It doesn't come easily to share openly what my heart has taken great care to guard for so long. The thought that someone may hear my most private thoughts and feel my most intimate feelings was horrifying to me. There is, however, great power in letting go and so this is what I have done.

Umbral talks of experiences and feelings that are not always welcomed with arms wide open. Child abuse, domestic violence, guilt, and depression aren't pleasant. There are many that would prefer that we turn a blind eye and keep quiet. We will not be silenced. Umbral expresses that there is an urgency to bring awareness in hopes that one day these will all be eradicated.

In addition to bringing awareness, Umbral brings attention to the relationship between women. Young and old women share a bond that isn't always leveraged as it should. I was raised by single mothers. My mother and her sisters raised their children together. Our elders demonstrated that it takes a village to raise children. They taught us that women need to have each other's back. We are to lift each other up when we are down. There should never be a reason why we can't complement each other. There should never be a reason to hate on one another. We are women, sisters, fierce, and a force to be reckoned with. We are stronger when we stand together.

There is one piece in particular that screams to the top of its lungs that queens call out to queens. **Sisterhood** is dedicated to Martha Rosa, Valerie Valencia, Katarina Andrea Ortiz, Milagros Estevez, Yajaira Garcia, Daisy Aviles, Alejandra Torres, Daniella Soto, Elisa Guillermo, Blacina Estevez, Kathy Talavera, Catherine Rodriguez Torres, Sheila Soto, Arianna Soto, Jenny Ramos, and Sophia Aida Cruz. Remember that you are fierce. You are beautiful. There is only one of you and that makes you a rare jewel. You are all queens. Wear your crown and walk with dignity.

There are other pieces within Umbral that were inspired by people who are important to me. **We were** is dedicated to my cousin Lazarus Rosa. We share awkwardness, heartbreak, and deep sadness. Our hearts can speak to each other. **Nameless** is dedicated to my sister Milagros Estevez. Always remember that God gives the hardest battles to His strongest soldiers. **Vintage Wine** is dedicated to Daniel Estevez. Your love is like fine wine. **The Last Remaining Queen** is dedicated to my aunt Carmen Reyes Carrillo. You gave me a name when my father deemed me unworthy of an identity. **The Last Prince** is dedicated to my little brother Efrain Soto, Jr. You were mommy's little prince and her gift to me.

Umbral is a summary of my life. Of the thoughts and feelings that dwell within me. My greatest desire is that it provokes changes and that it touches someone, somewhere who may feel hopeless.

About the Author

The author is an artist born and raised in Brooklyn, New York. She is the founder and CEO of Brain Junk LLC. Umbral is her first book. The collection of poetry and sketches attempt to bring awareness to issues such as child abuse, domestic violence, survivors' guilt, depression, struggles with personal image and heartbreak.